I0062184

HR MATTERS FOR CANNABIS COMPANIES

Renzie L. Richardson

Copyright © 2020 All
Rights Reserved
ISBN: 978-1-7348186-1-1

DEDICATION

To my children, Erika, Daphne and Quentin (Half-pint, Dew and Q-tip). You inspire me to live beyond my age.

ACKNOWLEDGMENT

I want to thank my family, friends, and clients who supported this project with their time and encouragement. I could not have done it without you.

ABOUT THE AUTHOR

Renzie Richardson is an entrepreneur and HR professional. She is passionate about training, coaching, and helping business owners and CEOs to understand talent economics in building profitable businesses.

For over 20 years, Renzie has been helping CEOs and business owners to understand the value of human resources, and she excels at leading, influencing, and building high performing teams.

Her clients are CEOs and business owners in the federal, commercial, and non-profit markets. They hire her to fix mistakes, improve human capital, or to implement strategies to improve profits and performance.

The information shared in this book offers a valuable understanding of human resources and how the discipline protects and influences the bottom line. Whether you are rolling in millions, lost missions, or aspire to make your first million, this book is for you!

PREFACE

In this book 'Why HR Matters,' we intend to draw a holistic perspective on the dynamic role of an HR function in the cannabis industry. As the widespread legalization of cannabis has gained momentum, entrepreneurs and business owners need to have the support of a knowledgeable, experienced HR professional to steer the legal landscape. If you want to stay in business and lead the cannabis market, you need to stay abreast of the government regulations at the national, state, and federal level.

An HR division ensures that compliance issues are also taken care of so that the smooth running of the business can be guaranteed. Tackling the internal and external environment is of utmost importance for a cannabis business, and this book will equip you to ensure that all the facets of HR-related work are taken care of duly. These include avoiding HR risks and wrongdoings, hiring and onboarding procedures, payroll and banking practices assigning job roles and responsibilities, performance management and training, and employee retention.

This resource will get you to reflect on whether your organization needs an HR professional and evaluate whether it is time to hire one yet.

CONTENTS

CHAPTER 1

A NEW FRONTIER

Over the years, social standards and considerations for alternative treatment for certain types of illnesses have invited acceptance after proving their benefits in the medical field. One of the most notable changes is that cannabis, aka marijuana, is no longer tabooed. Despite the exponential legalization of illegal drugs, especially in the western states, there is still a steady competition in the sale of cannabis in the legal and black markets. Nevertheless, prospective opportunities for growth in the legal cannabis industry can be significantly expected in the upcoming years.

The legal sale of cannabis is being lobbied for additional legalization and supported by certain federal and regulatory policies to stabilize the growth of this newly established cannabis industry and support social justice policies to discourage unauthorized dealings of cannabis. The vaping crisis was a significant blow to the overall revenue generated by the cannabis industry, which was estimated to account for 29% of the US legal cannabis sales and almost $4.9 billion in 2019.[1] Nevertheless, forecasts have predict-

---

[1]Hudock, C, (2019), 'As Smoke Clears from 2019, the US Cannabis Market Focuses on 2020'

ed a \$30 billion growth by 2025.[2] With currently only 12 countries permitting the legal cultivation of cannabis, it is highly possible the rest of the 46 counties have decided to lift the ban as well, which will greatly contribute to the prospering cannabis industry. Subsequently, 2020 has been marked as a turning point for legal cannabis in the US. With the widespread legalization, local agencies and the Federal Law have also shifted their attention to refining regulations and permitting issuance. The greater part of the authorization procedure is ensuring the compliance of the companies with the law, considering that the black market is still a stable and robust business.

Governments, attracted by the generous tax amounts they will receive, are working to bring an end to the unregulated sale of cannabis all over the US. However, resistance is expected in the smooth transitioning to the regulated market for which many enforcement actions are in practice. This will be highly evident in the state of California because of the presence of about 3000 illegal cannabis businesses that are the most significant potential threat to the regular market. Also, lucrative illicit markets tend to prove more successful than any enforcement techniques.

The black market is not the only target of enforcement policies; the legal dealers already in the business are also subjected to increased scrutiny. Local enforcement teams have previously announced stricter timely audits and inspections to certify and guarantee cooperation with the new policies and regulations. The main focus would be complaint-driven, opportunistic, or license renewal.

---

[2] Steinfeld, A, (2020), '*5 Cannabis Trends to Watch in 2020*'

Many recent cases show the enforcement actions taken against illegal dealers, especially against the entrepreneurs running their business in the legal market. The Battle Mountain Genetics case displays the companies' unorganized procedural claims to secure a permit and license even before the sale of cannabis had been legalized in California. During the initial months from January to April 2018, the company had no worker's compensation insurance for its employees. The Labor Commissioner's Office filed a complaint, and the company was demanded to pay a hefty fine of $35,196 calculated according to the weekly insurance cost.

The company did not comply with any of the orders and did not even pay the penalty. Battle Mountain Genetics was filed as a business with the California Secretary of State's Office in September 2016, and due to failure to meet tax requirements, the Franchise Tax Board suspended further business activities of the company. Later on, Sunset Island Group Inc. got ownership of the company in return for 50 million stock shares, and now it wholly belongs to VBF Brands.[3]

Besides taxation policies, a lot of cases where licenses were rescinded can also be observed. One such case was the Elite Care Company that was the first permissible provider in San Luis Obispo County to provide patients in the city. Only a year later, the business was shut down over a warehouse in Arroyo Grande, and all their deliveries were force-stopped. The contradiction of a policy from the Bureau of Cannabis Control and the Arroyo Grande City Ordinance led the two owners of Elite Care to lose their local permit to operate. The owners got a temporary license to provide over 400 of its patients the medicinal drugs that they

---

[3] Marino, P, (2019), 'Cannabis grower hit with $35,000 penalty for failing to carry worker's compensation insurance.'

required until the license expired. During that time, they could not come up with a way to resolve the issue and be forced to move somewhere else.[4]

Keeping in mind that cannabis is an emerging industry, the strict measures are somewhat justified. Nevertheless, it can be very challenging for potential operators and dealers to run their business smoothly. Succeeding and sustaining in the cannabis industry is no small feat and is indeed challenging in the current market. From technological advancements, government regulations, legalization, and the like, the cannabis industry has seen a lot in the last year. 2019 was marked with significant changes in the cannabis industry in the form of new State licensing, new job opportunities, multi-state expansions, acquisitions, and mergers, to name a few. Technology systems have been put in place to ensure smooth running and synchronization of different facets of a business. Special attention has been paid to human resources (HR) insights due to widespread cannabis legalization, which we shall discuss in detail.

When you are part of such a dynamic business scenario, it is imperative that a holistic perspective is considered when managing the different departments of the business and making critical decisions that will affect the company's different facets. Every business tries to stay abreast of the challenges that they may encounter, and hence, sound knowledge, awareness, and thorough research and development is vital. Apart from the regulation and legalization aspect, the cannabis industry has a lot of other frontiers to face as the federal government intervenes to enact national laws to govern and stabilize the industry. CEOs and business

---

[4] Leslie, K, (2018), 'SLO County's first permitted marijuana business shut down over warehouse dispute.'

owners need to understand the gravity of these challenging situations and realize the steps that need to be taken to maintain compliance and sustainability of their business.

Every year, players in the cannabis industry take ardent steps to set new precedents, achieve greater milestones in terms of profitability and market share, and have evolved in ways not predicted by industry experts. Preparing for the future is inevitable as compliance standards become stricter by the day, and industry competition is becoming more overwhelming. The challenges abounding the cannabis industry are only expected to increase in the future years. Therefore, owners and entrepreneurs are advised to equip themselves with the most relevant knowledge and technology breakthroughs to combat talent and financial challenges that may help them scale their business. If you have a cannabis business that is not under the supervision of a qualified, certified HR professional, it's time to consider hiring one. Until your HR policies are aligned across the spectrum, your business's chances of being exposed to practices that are not legal expose you to fines, and the risk of losing your license to operate. A well-defined HR and talent management strategy can help you survive in an industry that is in flux and to stave off risks of investigations, litigations, and fines.

Challenges for the Cannabis Industry

As aforementioned, I believe that CEOs and business owners need to mind their Ps and Qs and realize the part they play in the sustainability of their business and the industry. As a PROSCI certified business coach, I provide HR consulting, training, and coaching services to help mid-sized business owners, woman-owned, and minority owners build successful organizations leveraging talent economics and strategic development. Our consulting services for cannabis markets include human management, training, leadership development, executive coaching, change management, and employee engagement. We connect the dots and help our clients to stay connected and up-to-date with state and federal laws and updates.

Value of Human Resources

Since cannabis has been accepted as a legal substance to produce, market, and sell openly in the nation's economy, it has posed a huge challenge for employers. Previously, it was sold illegally through underhanded means, and employers did not need to make policy accommodations in the workplace. In light of the imminent government legislation regarding workforce rules and policies, employers will have to ensure that employee rights are considered without compromising equal opportunities, fair wages, and other HR practices that are characteristic of legally operated businesses. Cannabis farmers now have this responsibility, along with storefront owners, as well as all levels of management governing the industry to ensure employees are taken care of with due respect and regard. These include, but are not limited to, hiring and firing decisions (preferably on merit), training, employee engagement, and job satisfaction. Trust me, these practices are well worth the investment and attention in an industry that is plagued by a talent deficit and legal scrutiny amid resource poaching abound the cannabis landscape.

Hiring and Employee Engagement

According to a report, the cannabis industry has created 211,000 jobs across the US, out of which 64,000 of these were recently updated in the year 2018.[5] These figures give us a fair view of the viability of this field.

If the cannabis industry were to grow at the same pace with leaps and bounds, much pressure would be placed on the HR leaders to ensure that they keep up with the ever-growing workforce. This is because it needs to be managed in a way that helps build long-term sustainability. Cannabis has lately become a growing industry with businesses relying on passionate, self-trained labor as it lacks formal education. One of the biggest HR dilemmas includes hiring employees that are a 'good fit' for the job and also complement your business brand. A thorough talent management program will benefit your organization and ensure your recruiting efforts are made as efficiently as possible, support employee retention, and align employee onboarding with the business goals. Although turnover cannot be completely mitigated, HR challenges need to be addressed head-on so that cannabis business owners and entrepreneurs do not suffer.

Compliance Issues

The cannabis industry is undoubtedly one of the most highly regulated industries in the USA. This puts all business owners and entrepreneurs operating in the cannabis realm to ensure compliance right down to the smallest detail. On top of that, compliance measures are constantly evolving, putting businesses in a state of limbo. Constant changes in compliance procedures leave companies with no option but to adjust to new standard reporting, products, equipment, and procedures. Not only are there industry-specific compliance issues that HR tracks and reports, but many

---

[5] Barcott, B, (2019), 'As of 2019, legal cannabis has created 211,000 full-time jobs in America'

are also related to employee safety and wellbeing. Of the safety and anti-discrimination laws to FMLA (family and medical leave), it is essential to stay on top of all the regulations and compliance issues.

Also, cannabis managers have had to deal with the myriad of hours and wage laws, rest breaks, meal times, and overtime laws. The prospect for compliance is a major challenge for frontline leaders in an ever-changing industry as business owners aspire to grow and prosper. Staying abreast of all these compliance laws and procedures is a must.

Legalization and Social Justice Implications

Operating in the cannabis industry, as a business owner, you should be aware of the hot-button issues in state legislatures. One such program that attempts to amend incarceration with social justice offers black and brown people the opportunity to expunge arrests associated with marijuana or cannabis for employment or offer entrepreneurship funding. These types of social justice programs help offenders to enter the regulated marijuana market and recognize communities disproportionately affected by violence, unemployment, poverty, divestment, and criminal activities. In some states, employers have been successfully hiring offenders in cultivation jobs to earn a living legally instead of making money in the black market.

Banking Opportunity Barriers

Businesses within the cannabis industry face resistance when it comes to federal regulators and media issues. As per the Insurance Journal, the biggest obstacles come from this area, which is further worsened by different regulations. Cannabis businesses are not given the free hands or right to work in collaboration with banks that are federally insured, which deters everyday operations and hence delays things. Private funders continue to dominate the scene. Cannabis-friendly financial support is tough to find in the current federal Schedule I listing of cannabis.

Since banking poses such a significant hindrance, quite a few vendors steer clear of this industry altogether as they dread the federal legal state of cannabis. Even widely-acceptable and re-nowned payroll providers like Paylocity and ADP are staying far away from this industry.

Cash Transactions

Since the banking industry is giving such a tough time to can-nabis business owners and entrepreneurs, many of the businesses are left with no option but to carry out their operations based on cash. This further complicates the system of borrowing and lend-ing from banks since there is no credit record, affecting the credit rating of the business owner. The federal government considers cannabis to be a drug, which is why many banks come under this restriction of not being able to pass loans or accept money from any cannabis-related business as it gets classified under the cate-gory of money laundering. If you are looking forward to work with any bank insured by the FDIC, this is a common source of concern. Likewise, it can be justifiably said that the likelihood of integration of the banking system in the cannabis industry is high-ly dependent on federal regulations.

Medical Community Stigma

Despite the legalization and widespread use of cannabis and medical marijuana by health care facilities and doctors, a vast majority of the public has still not come around to accept this anomaly. They still believe that these drugs should be illegal as it instills addiction and other unwanted habits in people. Hospitals are denied federal funding if they promote cannabis in any way. This stigma in hospitals is one of the serious challenges that cannabis business owners and entrepreneurs should keep in mind before delving into unchartered waters. It's all a matter of time when one federal regulation can make or break your business. Challenges are real in the cannabis realm.

Contrary to popular belief, many growers and processors of cannabis believed that the legalization of recreational and medical marijuana or cannabis would mean that compliance regulations would also be relaxed. However, the scenario seems even more taxing than they were before. If consumer demand increases, the market for cannabis will also automatically increase the state and federal level regulations.

The struggles don't stop here; with so many cannabis entrepreneurs starting businesses in the cannabis industry to capitalize on the lucrative market opportunities, challenges are abounding. Local and multi-state licenses have become an additional hurdle along with additional facility authorizations.

Looking Forward to Growth in the Cannabis Industry

Despite many and completely legitimate challenges in the cannabis industry and individual businesses as such, the market is worth the effort to establish policies and practices in keeping with compliance issues and managing a profitable business. If you are a cannabis business owner or even a budding entrepreneur trying to establish yourself in this industry, recognize the presence of these challenges. The cannabis industry is a lucrative industry, and professional assistance can do wonders in helping you nip the problem in the bud.

In the future, the cannabis industry requires rigorous HR practices and policies to be implemented to make business operations more profitable. Cannabis businesses are in dire need of tools and resources that will equip them to duly keep track of crucial compliance data, keep the management updated with recent regulatory deadlines and policies, identify and mitigate any operational inefficiencies, and overlook the decision-making process to ensure maximum success. Human Resource functions in the cannabis industry are much more than simply hiring and firing decisions, salary, and benefits. The process of finding the right fit is crucial in the cannabis industry as employers who perform "plant-touching" jobs need to be well-versed with the laws and policies to ensure safety and compliance. Furthermore, federal law requires all employers to comply with standard federal laws such as e-Verify and Equal Employment Opportunity (EEO).

I happened to attend an annual cannabis convention, and one session I attended was the investors' panel Q & A. The session was somewhat informal to offer attendees an opportunity to ask questions. The attendees asked questions about money, and the panelist expressed more interest in risks. One of the investors surprised me with this response: "When I evaluate a company, I drill down to look at people, processes, and systems. I measure risk based on policies, practices, turnover, and how the company manages the money. These are trigger points that imply a high burn rate through funding and a low return on investment."

The panel of investors offered quite a few sobering insights – as lucrative as the industry is, foolish deals are not the driving force. A high return on investment (ROI) is the going rate. Hence, it can be justifiably said that investors in the cannabis industry also carry out a holistic audit of your company in terms of everything from policies and practice to the financials. This book is an attempt to lay certain things on the table so that cannabis businesses are better prepared to set their cannabis business on a firm footing.

I am writing this book to increase awareness of business owners and CEOs of what they need to do to up their game and not fall prey to requirements and changing laws. After all, in this highly competitive industry with limited licensing, why take the risk? The industry has gained momentum, and with HR professionals to smooth out operations within the industry, business owners and CEOs can sail through these challenging times with the right tools and people, while harnessing a solid foundation. By the end of the book, I aim to paint a non-biased picture of the cannabis industry so that business owners and entrepreneurs can benefit from it.

CHAPTER 2

WHY HR MATTERS

Human Resource (HR) has an indispensable role in the cannabis industry, one that can be considered specific and necessary. Despite the crucial part that HR plays in navigating through the myriad of federal and state laws, many cannabis business owners fail to recognize the growing importance of HR to their business. Unfortunately, non-compliance with employment laws is one of the major factors that cannabis businesses are levied fines and is one aspect that needs prompt action to fix.

The crux of the situation is, as would be the case for any organization with more than five employees, the need and existence of a human resource department becomes an absolute necessity. When talking in particular about a cannabis business, the role of HR is central in looking after and battling legal nuances that need to be duly addressed to ensure smooth business operations. The US Department of Labor routinely conducts audits of cannabis companies to ensure that they comply with labor, pay, and employment laws. Failure to conform to the rules and policies may lead to the business license being revoked or enforcement of whatever penalty the law allows.

Absence or lack of HR in the Cannabis Industry

Since the legalization of Cannabis, the industry is still relatively new, and there are quite a few areas that need attention. Entrepreneurs and business owners are still trying to figure out their way around what works in this industry and what doesn't. Amidst all these struggles, HR is often neglected expertise in the business as company owners are unable to gauge the gravity of HR matters. The ever-shifting laws and regulations present a legitimate set of challenges that need to be taken seriously when operating your cannabis business.

CEOs of smaller cannabis companies often try to overlook the requirement of setting up an HR department by trying to take on the role of HR themselves. They fail to realize that trying to juggle between their own responsibilities and looking after other environmental factors becomes taxing, and there's only so much that is humanly possible. Most CEOs do not possess the technical expertise or the relevant background and experience to post legal job ads, recruit, hire, fire, manage, and manage all HR operations. Hiring and firing decisions may seem to be very easy and straightforward on its face, but actually have a lot of legalities and defensive strategies behind it. It's a huge legal pitfall plaguing the cannabis industry when CEOs and business owners, whose work is to develop and implement the business plan, are involved in work like HR-related or administrative decisions. They're not trained or programmed to work in that capacity, and it is more advantageous to retain these core competencies and outsource this function of the business to the experts in their respective domains.

As a business owner or CEO, you don't want to expose your company to risks in the way you deal with HR-related matters in terms of your decisions and how you communicate your actions.

An HR professional knows how to make the best decision in the interest of the company, and makes decisions that mitigate risk and are defensible. A lack of knowledge or spending money on expensive legal advice for routine HR functions is misappropriated. A competent HR professional will mitigate risks that require legal counsel. A professional understands how to partner with legal counsel to develop a defensible position should a problem that involves legal proceedings emerges.

The Importance of HR in the Cannabis Industry

If you haven't considered hiring a trained and expert HR professional or outsourcing this function, you would want to consider it an immediate priority. The cannabis industry is faced with critical HR issues such as recruiting and retaining talent in this booming sector with a high demand for workers. While these dilemmas are the tip of the iceberg, other HR matters involve a plethora of other issues that evolve with the ever-changing employment laws and pay issues.

If you are operating in the cannabis industry, riding the tide of changing regulations and opportunities is a part of the normal routine. Whether you are cultivating plants, manufacturing products, or running a dispensary, the landscape is exploding with opportunities and rising HR concerns. As of 2019, recent stats show that the cannabis industry employed over 211,000 full-time employees in the United States, and projected to add nearly 35,000 new jobs in 2020 – staggering growth that is forecast to double in the next two years. In addition to the expanding landscape in the emerging US markets, rapid hiring causes another challenge when employers set aside hiring guidelines to onboard talent quickly to meet industry demands. The Human Resource (HR) function is not only about hiring and firing but also encompasses real-time tracking of employees, background checks, offer letters, PTO policies, payroll management, employee classifications, and various other tasks.

This helps mobilize the workforce and ensure a smooth onboarding and integrating new employees to ramp up quickly. Business owners need to make sure that they hire employees in compliance with legal documentation. This is not only because it is a federal requirement but also because employees represent your company brand and need to be acquired and trained to represent the company and perform critical business competencies.

From setting up a cannabis business to successfully running it and optimizing ROI, business owners and entrepreneurs in the cannabis industry face a multitude of challenges when it comes to managing a workforce. Employers are held responsible for complying with the applicable wage and hour laws, working on ethical anti-discrimination laws, establishing benefit plans, protecting the goodwill, administering leaves, and any other overlapping laws that may put the business operations in jeopardy. The importance of HR cannot be stressed enough.

Areas of Common Legal Pitfalls in the Cannabis Industry

Want to steer clear of legal trouble? Here are five of the most common mistakes laypeople make:

Wrong Hire: Business owners and entrepreneurs often fall for hiring friends, relatives, or wrong candidates. They forego the importance of vetting for recruitment, especially in an industry like this one, and fail to conduct extensive background checks and standard hiring procedures. The money spent on a bad hire is 30% of hiring a part-time HR professional.

No Job Descriptions: As much as it seems that business owners are shifting to an "open, more relaxed" workplace, job descriptions are much needed to tell your employees specifically what you expect of them. You can't possibly determine if the candidate is the right hire and best fit without a mutual agreement about expectations.

No Performance Planning & Documentation. The most common mistake business owners and CEOs fail to do is conduct performance reviews, meetings, and documents, whether good or bad. If there are claims or allegations involving performance problems, business owners and CEOs fail their burden of proof because they overlook this matter, and put yourself at risk for more expensive legal actions.

Ignoring Employment Laws: When they hire friends, family, or anyone else, business owners make the mistake of negating employment laws that are designed to protect their interests and employees. When you exercise ignorance or intentional disregard for the law, misunderstanding will not protect you from legal action or problems that may arise.

Improper Classification: So often, I have seen business owners and entrepreneurs hire independent contractors, but they make a costly mistake by treating them like employees. It's a common practice for businesses to hire contract employees to save money and to sidestep hiring employee requirements, but oftentimes the risk of violating DOL and IRS requirements may come back to haunt you when there is a dispute about pay and work conditions.

Simply put, employment law is not easily understood by a layman. An option is to carve out time from growing the business and invest in your training to manage critical HR and payroll functions. A comprehensive program to equip you to make legal HR decisions include:

- Human Resources Management & Understanding of the HR function.
- Talent Acquisition & Selecting Employees.
- Payroll & HRIS Systems.
- Health & Safety
- Performance Management
- Training & Development
- Employment Law
- Harassment & Inclusion

The comprehensive list of competencies is a great way to start to become more aware of how HR matters protect your company.

The Search for Quality Candidates

We talk at length about how HR continues to lead the organization towards success. With the ever-expanding roles in the cannabis industry, HR efforts become all the more highlighted. When recruiting the 'right fit' for the right job, HR doesn't only need to ensure that recruitment is done on an ongoing and routine basis, but compliance is also maintained. According to a trusted source, the Cannabis Business Times, discriminatory job postings are identified as a risk and pose lawsuits by women, disabled, older, and minority workers. What these company's fail to realize is that hiring policies and practices that limit the equal opportunity to protected groups can lead to violating anti-discrimination laws.

Poorly worded job advertisements are one of the most common mistakes that cannabis companies make. Without formal HR education, many cannabis owners end up drafting illegal job postings. Who is to be blamed for all this? Only a dedicated HR professional can understand these types of risks and mitigating strategies to protect the company. HR information system (HRIS) software can aid and automate the applicant tracking and hiring, including job listings compliant to equal opportunity rules and guidelines. The hunt for candidates is also broken down into simpler steps as it is integrated with several job boards across the continuum, including social media.

Hiring

It goes without saying that you need to have stringent rules and policies around your hiring process. You cannot have lossy-goosy procedures that may expose loopholes, which can altogether ruin your entire cannabis business. Hiring is one of the most crucial and decisive stages that need to be in compliance with local and state employment laws as its practice shapes the perception employees develop when starting their work relationship with your company – what is the message you convey about your company? Your credibility rests on first impressions during the first 90 days and how this period is structured to set up new employees for success.

A proper HR function ensures that your new hire documentation and practices follow the criteria expected by state and federal laws and protects you from anti-discrimination employment laws. BHFL Group starts with a comprehensive interview checklist that lists requirements and record notes to profile the candidate interview. Our approach is conversational but minimizes the chances of asking illegal questions that can increase the likelihood of discriminatory complaints.

Cannabis hiring managers are in constant competition to find candidates with the right skills, and it is becoming more challenging with the ever-changing laws. HR professionals understand this landscape and utilize tactics to promote the company brand to attract and retain highly sought-after talent. By 2025, it is expected that 1.63 million legal cannabis jobs will saturate the job market, according to New Frontier Data.[6]

Workplace Policy Manual

What is the first thing that comes to your mind when you hear workplace policy manual? Common sense says it's a comprehensive set of rules and procedures that governs your operations and day-to-day activities. It is imperative to have an employee handbook in place well before you launch your operations to avoid pitfalls that may sabotage your efforts and put your business at risk of attracting investors, losing clientele, and losing business opportunities. The employee handbook should comply with all federal, state, and local employment laws, some of which are prerequisites for acquiring a business license.

A comprehensive employee handbook can give a sense of direction to all your managers and employees of all levels alike. This manual sets the guidelines for how you work, interact, perform, and comply with internal and external standards. Ideally, the manual should encompass a comprehensive list of policies pertaining to (not inclusive of all):

---

[6]*US Federal Cannabis Legalization Could Be Worth $128.8 Billion in Taxes and 1.6 Million Jobs* https://www.businesswire.com/news/home/20191002005609/en/U.S.-Federal-Cannabis-Legalization-Worth-128.8-Billion

- Payroll procedures
- Holidays
- Insurance
- Training
- Absences
- Dress code
- Anti-harassment and anti-discrimination mechanisms
- Complaint management
- Employee evaluations
- Sexual harassment laws
- Drug policies at the workplace
- Termination and lay-offs
- Employee-employer relationship management

Human Resource professionals offer the necessary knowledge and experience to interpret and regulate these areas. They ensure consistency between written policies and business practices.

Employee Turnover

The majority of the cannabis companies operating in a lucrative economy are more focused on managing profit and revenue loss. Finance dominates a major part of the firm's operations, and any expenses that are likely to reduce the window of revenues often get side-tracked. Unfortunately, HR is one of those expenditures developing companies are reluctant to invest in. This is primarily due to the misunderstandings and perceptions that HR is an overhead cost vs. a cost savings strategy.

BHFL Group partners with our clients to show value in how we are a cost savings center by mitigating risk and loss as it pertains to talent economics.

The truth of the matter is, when leveraged wisely, human resources for cannabis business owners can actually help save costs in the long run.

The employer strategies for recruiting, vetting, hiring, onboarding, and training are not an overnight development. It takes the investment of time and resources to engage an employee to the level where they are productive and contributes to the company's profitability. Let's assume that it costs you around $7,000 over a six-month duration to train an employee to be fully engaged. Without a strategic approach, the intangible cost can be as much as $20,000. Disengagement costs employers billions of dollars annually.

Now imagine a worst-case scenario where even after the six-month training period, the employee decides to resign after the investment of time, money, and resources?

With the growth of job opportunities in the cannabis industry at a staggering rate, the market favors employees – a shopper's market. Unhappy employees have a wealth of opportunities to find employers that offer them work, benefits, and perks that are important for maintaining their lifestyle. Employees crave appreciation and want a rewarding job that is more than a paycheck. Employers need retention strategies that incentivize loyalty and career growth, such as various training programs, performance bonuses, positive feedback, and succession planning that offer career growth and advancement.

Having said that, if you calculate the cost of losing a valuable employee that you invested six months of your time, in addition to the salary investment – you're clearly at a loss. Not only have you $14,000 in recruiting and onboarding, but you also lost a valuable asset in human capital that impacts your bottom line. Besides, losing a valuable asset is an additional investment of revenue for vetting, hiring, and training a new employee, which is no guarantee whether they will stick around or not. Having an experienced HR professional will not eliminate turnover, but their expertise in employee relations and job satisfaction can anticipate issues that erode the company's capabilities to perform and excel. No matter how lucrative the cannabis industry might be, if your company's burn rate through revenue and contribute to low-profit margin, human resources is a valuable business strategy that can help contain loss.

Conclusion: HR Does Matter

With the near future of the cannabis industry expecting federal legislation to come, investing in a dedicated human resource can help business owners or CEOs to navigate through the rough waters and scale their operations. The best position is to solidify your company with an HR strategy that promotes the best talent to capitalize on the opportunities presented by the market, in the light of legalization.

It's all about riding the wave equipped with the best of HR tools and practices so that you can exercise the flexibility and adaptability to change. Cannabis business owners and entrepreneurs envisioning themselves to stay in the market for the duration need to hone their business strategies when it comes to acquiring, training, and retaining top-notch talent. HR as a business strategy will is an advantage when it comes to mitigating challenges related to talent shortages and bridging the skills gap. Cannabis business owners and CEOs have an understanding of how talent attracts investors. This business strategy implies a stable organization positioned for sustainable growth and ROI.

Strengthening your business with an experienced HR professional will address critical HR matters. As the industry takes a role in legislating laws that impact the cannabis industry, it is crucial to take the necessary measures to ensure your business is prepared for the long haul. BHFL Group recommends evaluating HR options to select the best solution for your HR needs. If you do not want to hire a full-time employee, consider retainer agreement or outsource your need to a PEO (Professional Employee Organization). The most important decision in a business is to hire an experienced HR professional!

Having an HR strategy for your company is not only important to manage your internal policies and procedures. Your HR strategy also protects the company from lawsuits and complaints that can be managed through policies, procedures, and practices.

Additionally, your leadership team and employees will know what is expected of them. The right HR professional can enhance your company brand and is an added bonus to the CEO and business owner.

Take a look at the reasons you don't want to hire an HR professional and measure your reasons against the risk if you don't – what is your next move?

CHAPTER 3
AVOIDING HR RISKS & WRONGDOING

With employers entering a new decade, a whole new wave of HR risks and compliance burdens need to be tackled to make sure your ship is able to sail and navigate turbulent times in the cannabis industry. The human resources function contributes to the efficient running of the organization in innumerable ways ranging from establishing the company talent brand to strategic planning and implementing policies and practices. If your senior and mid-level leaders are well-trained in HR matters, their leadership of the workforce strengthens your company's capabilities and facilitate your employees' capacity in a number of ways.

The business functions that HR manages can significantly elevate the employees' perceptions and overall experience with your company, all the while establishing and consolidating your HR operations. Irrespective of your business industry, the HR function is indispensable and necessary on its own. Let's examine the crucial role of HR from a holistic perspective before we see it exclusively through the lens of a cannabis owner or entrepreneur.

Strategy Development and Management

Human resources experts realize that human capital, training, and performance management can lead an organization to unprecedented success. Understanding this strategy, the HR function aims to directly impact ROI and bottom line by influencing the strategic direction that takes into account the company's current and future talent needs. With the use of different assessment tools and succession planning, human capital requirements are anticipated based on market demands and competitive advantage. Experienced HR professionals make sure they have a seat at the table to play their part in corporate decision-making to stay on top of the company's human resource needs and to manage the strategies to avoid negative outcomes.

Avoid Liability Issues

In the fast-paced digital age, it is challenging to manage a variety of risk factors involved in managing a business single-handedly. As a function of human resources, employee relations help negate risks associated with managing and correcting employee behavior. This function helps mitigate interpersonal conflict that can escalate to arbitration or formal legal proceedings, which frequently discover the unlawful or inconsistent application of state and federal laws. As much as human capital is the lifeblood of any business, it can pose a significant risk in corrective and monetary damages for employers.

HR experts are trained in the art of employee relations and resolving internal conflict to mitigate escalation that may require external legal solutions, and state or federal oversight. Not having an experienced HR practitioner to take care of this aspect exposes risks of tarnishing the company's reputation, investor interest, and profitability. Federal and state laws pertaining to harassment and discrimination deserve your undivided attention.

Compliance Maintenance

When it comes to ensuring compliance across all departments of a company, HR plays the role of a warrior. Armed with the recent laws and regulations closely guiding employment relationships, HR professionals are experienced in managing resistance and getting buy-in to protect the company. Uniform HR practices are a necessity to document hiring procedures, and compensation, promotion, and termination practices. Whether your business is in the private sector or you are a federal contractor, compliance is a necessity. Compliance includes EEO/AAP – written affirmative action plans, a proper applicant flow log, and disparity impact analyses. Other over-arching laws that regulate the employee-employer relationship regardless of the industry you operate in are briefly described below. Some major laws include:

- **Fair Labor Standards Act** – Under this Act, employee rights are preserved by protecting their entitlement to receive a certain minimum wage. This Act also establishes employee rights for over overtime payment and prohibits discrimination based on age, gender, race, or color. It also requires employers to pay covered employees who are not otherwise exempt at least the federal minimum wage and overtime pay of one-and-one-half-times the regular rate of pay.

- **Family and Medical Leave Act (FMLA)** – Employers with 50 or more employees are entitled to a maximum of 12 weeks of paid/unpaid medical leave based on federal and state laws. Furthermore, the employee has the right to be reinstated in the same or similar position before the leave commenced.

- **The Occupational Safety and Health (OSH) Act** – This Act mandates that employers must provide their employees with work and a workplace free from recognized, serious hazards. OSHA enforces the Act through workplace inspections and investigations.

- **Worker's Compensation** – Employers are required to carry worker's compensation insurance to mitigate the employee financial burden resulting from a workplace injury.

- **Uniform Services Employment and Reemployment Rights Act (USERRA)** – This protects the right of employees who are summoned for military duty to serve the nation.

Risk Mitigation

Risk comes in various forms and poses a threat to the company's bottom line from both external and internal sources. A simple HR risk could be the act of making a poor hiring decision. When deviations are practiced in recruiting, screening, and selecting candidates, the impact can infect and erode the company brand and overall organizational performance. This means that it is not only the individuals who suffer, but the team, workplace culture, organizational culture, and turnover are hugely impacted. A lot of workplace policies and procedures are in place to create continuity and to contain risks. Human resources' purpose is to ensure employees thrive in a healthy workplace and, in turn, be ambassadors to spread positive word-of-mouth about the company.

Training and Development

People are your most valuable asset. As cliché as it may sound, without the right people in the right job, your company will not be able to compete and be competitive. Success is like an illusion if you have substandard talent coupled with disengagement. Remember that it is quality and high-performing talent in your organization that ultimately help you achieve your target goals that are realized in the bottom line. This makes HR's role even more crucial in recruiting the right talent and training, developing, and retaining them. Building a tribe and getting employees to give the allegiance and alliance to a company is accomplished through building an experience that is more than a paycheck. Beyond the ability to earn a wage to afford their living standards, employees are looking for an opportunity to grow and add their footprint to a company that aspires to achieve meaningful outcomes. Highly motivated people are looking for career growth and value addition that has a positive impact on their life. If they are not trained, nurtured, and developed in the right capacity at the right time, they seek out opportunities elsewhere.

HR Policies and Compliance in the Cannabis Industry

At the core of the cannabis industry lies a commitment that focuses on serving on consumer satisfaction, financial modeling, brand monetization and development, and capital cadence. These are some top-notch business priorities that executives have on the top of their minds, but they often tend to miss out on the one grave matter that needs to be developed internally – human resources. Only with the setup and development of human resource practices come policies, structure, and compliance, As cannabis entities continue to grow in America, human resource experts are also having to adapt to navigate to emerging regulations that differ from state to state. The cannabis industry has its own set of unique challenges that need special attention, too. You can't follow the one blueprint in the cannabis industry as it varies for growers, retail, and medical sectors.

How do you know you are hiring the right talent for industry-specific jobs? How do you ensure compliance and that no laws are breached in the process? The industry requires business owners to keep cannabis compliance training at the forefront and leverage it to grow their business. Certain background checks are required for specific sectors before you can hire someone in certain cannabis jobs.

That's where we step in! Be it a small or medium-sized business; your talent goes a long way in laying the building blocks of your business. The BHFL Group will partner with you to provide robust, integrative solutions that laser-focus on our basic services inclusive of:

- Individual and executive coaching
- HR Consulting
- Training
- Leadership development
- Executive Coaching
- Change management
- Employee engagement

All this and much more with the help of our HR professionals, OD practitioners, trainers, and certified RCC/WABC coaches. Using an integrative approach, we equip individuals, leaders, and organizations to meet their targets and move yet another step closer to their dreams.

As an increasing number of states adopt the legalization of cannabis – not only medical marijuana, but recreational as well – opportunities are plentiful.

Under the Federal Law

It is to be noted that despite widespread legalization, at the federal level, the drug still remains illegal. It is viewed as a controlled substance, and the US Supreme Court has given the federal government the right to punish any violators of the law. Under the Controlled Substances Act (CSA), cannabis falls under the category of a Schedule I drug, which labels this drug as being extremely addictive and not passing off as a drug with medical value. Doctors are only allowed to "recommend" the use of cannabis under the First Amendment but cannot prescribe it.

Cannabis laws on a federal level are still quite severe. People found guilty of violating federal law faced serious repercussions. However, on this front, leading cannabis policy organizations and lobbyists are involved in policy and laws that govern the industry.

Under the State Laws

Despite the status of cannabis as a Schedule I controlled substance, big businesses in the States have legalized the use of cannabis as a recreational substance. The ambiguity regarding the legal status of marijuana (cannabis) has resulted in business owners operating in this niche struggling with unique business challenges and a future filled with uncertainties. Separate laws and regulations have been drafted by some states making recreational cannabis legal in hopes of expanding the market and types of consumers to partake. It is expected that more states will follow giving recreational cannabis the green light, which might give federal laws more involvement to standardize laws and usage. It can be justifiably said that despite cannabis being accepted socially, some of the most challenging business and compliance issues have been faced by cannabis owners and entrepreneurs. Employers have been unable to keep a uniform check on hiring, training, developing, and even retaining the brightest employees. As the workforce expands and with the prediction of the cannabis market rising to a $57 billion mark by 2027, it is but natural that challenges will increase in tandem.

The compliance landscape has been continuously evolving at a great pace. It is not a surprise that 33% of employers struggle with maintaining asynchrony with the State regulations. Irrespective of whether you are a small business owner who wears all the hats of HR or someone who is responsible for hiring several people in specific job roles every day, compliance is a significant responsibility. This is where HR can take on the role of leadership and provide technical expertise to manage this aspect of the business. If your business is found breaching any statutory or regulatory compliance, it could cost you valuable assets in the long run. In the end, it all boils down to the HR policies and best practices that will help prevent it. The HR function is formed primarily to take care of these issues and work in close collaboration with the business owner and the leadership team. They make sure that all of the managers and supervisors are on the same page and are well aware of the dire consequences of non-compliance. They make sure that all the training material and modules contain the necessary and crucial information needed to stay on top of HR-related goals.

These also include taking care of sexual harassment training and handling the company's image on social media, in addition to the right partner who can take complete responsibility and ensure compliance from inception to the implementation of policies, procedures, and practices.

Sexual Harassment Training

Sexual harassment in the workplace is not a new concept but has been around in different capacities and varying frequencies. This requires HR professionals to keep their eye on the target, not lose focus, and devise a proactive strategy to mitigate risk at an individual as well as organizational level. Policies should be all-encompassing and take into account anti-retaliation, anti-harassment, and anti-bullying policies alongside creating awareness for preventive measures. HR unquestionably stays abreast of the federal laws that apply to all forms of harassment in the workplace. This makes it necessary to have a workplace harassment prevention program to ensure a harassment-free work environment where employees feel safe and protected at all times.

Cannabis Industry in the Age of Social Media

The cannabis industry, on the whole, has undergone a few federal laws and plenty of state regulations. It hasn't managed to escape the clutches of social media, and it comes with its fair share of compliance rules. This definitely requires an expert to handle and avoid missteps that communicate a message that violates state and local laws. Since cannabis is a controlled substance, marketing and promoting your business require fully transparent strategies in its communications. Since social media is subject to public scrutiny, you need to be very careful out there and post well-articulated messages that do not breach any federal or state laws. There are certain restrictions on advertising for cannabis businesses where no ads are to target minors. TV and radio are completely banned. Cannabis businesses are required to give disclaimers and put an age restriction on their content alongside remaining compliant to those setting the laws. E-commerce alone is not a very viable platform for the cannabis industry, so a push strategy to increase sales using social media is key. A traditional retail approach is so not the way to go for cannabis brands either; in fact, it is advised that retailers take a more education-centric and lifestyle approach so that the target buyers are attracted to become consumers.

These are in addition to the usual challenges marketers face to use social media to get traction, visitors, engagement, and ultimately conversions. Turning your social media account into a strategy as a cannabis business owner or entrepreneur is no small feat in order to stay clear of all the social media rules and the legal compliance issues. One successful approach is shifting the focus from "hard-selling" to providing value-adding real-time information. However, it goes unsaid that whoever manages your social media should be knowledgeable and supervised by a team that knows the legal environment surrounding the cannabis industry. HR policies and procedures keep a holistic check on everything that affects business operations. Establishing regulations are not at all done overnight. It requires a certain level of collaboration, choosing the right platforms to disseminate information, and implementing the right tools and parameters to ensure that the right audience receives your message.

BHFL is a one-stop solution to all your HR needs, whereby our team of specialists and consultants understand the role of HR function influence operation policies in other disciplines, such as marketing. We boast an impressive track record of assisting and facilitating entrepreneurs and small and mid-sized companies for

30 years to help scale and grow their business in private and federal markets. From the perspective that we have put forth, HR will become a more valued discipline in helping the cannabis industry navigate through turbulent times and ensure compliance at all levels. The opportunity is real and multi-faceted. Workforce management and human capital are leading this industry. If the industry is to grow at its anticipated rate, human resource needs to play a role in its growth.

There are certain cardinal principles that every cannabis business owner and entrepreneur would benefit from knowing. Now that you realize how imperative the role of HR is let's delve deeper into what lies in store for the cannabis industry!

CHAPTER 4

SIX THINGS EVERY CANNABIS COMPANY NEEDS TO KNOW

According to Business Insider, the lucrative cannabis industry garnered funding of $2.3 billion alone through VCs in 2019. This marked a significant $0.8 billion increase from the previous year. With the legal environment surrounding the cannabis industry being highly volatile and constantly-evolving, business owners are struggling to adjust and set up their establishments on firm grounds.

We can justifiably say that the legal status of recreational and medical marijuana is in constant flux and varies from state to state, as we saw in the previous chapter. This presents a plethora of mind-altering opportunities and risks that businesses need to be aware of.

If you're an aspiring entrepreneur or business enthusiast look-ing forward to becoming a part of the *'Green Rush,'* you're most likely inclined to become involved in a booming and highly profit-able industry. Whenever a new industry presents opportunities and growth to entrepreneurial enthusiasts, it's a whole new world of dreams with obviously some element of risk aversion. However, with the cannabis industry in context, the rules and regulations are quite complicated as compared to other sectors. Amongst a host of challenges, as a business owner, you need to sail through various social, legal, and financial issues.

Overview of the Cannabis Industry as a Lucrative Business Opportunity

Even though cannabis has not yet achieved the status of being legal at a federal level, it is one of the most provocative and exciting industries to invest in and grow. With being legalized in most US states, it not only serves as potential investment opportunities but also qualifies as a vertical that can leverage the power of technology to scale their business.

Everything from analytics to the Internet's capabilities can be embedded in the business model of a cannabis firm to help it reach target customers and achieve unprecedented growth. If we talk about the landscape of US states, it can be noted that natural alternatives to traditional pharmaceuticals are on the rise. Various medical conditions are cured with medical marijuana programs such as cancer, pain relief, psychiatric, and neurological disorders. Cannabis has the potential to be the next big legal recreational material after caffeine, alcohol, and tobacco. Other industries that stem out of this major cannabis market include byproducts and other related manufacturing firms such as green plastics, biofuel, cooking oil, and hemp fibers for upholstery, clothing, and other fabric use. Complimentary industries such as the likes of industrial, agricultural, and technology sectors are a great boost to the growing cannabis industry as a whole.

The cannabis industry has matured from a license-aggregation phase through a product innovation phase to a market share-grabbing phase – to be finally met with the execution phase. To build a more robust and efficient framework for industry growth, one must stay connected as a cannabis fraternity.

Analyze Your Financial Environment and Prospects

Getting funding can be a struggle in any industry you are operating in, but it is more of a challenge for cannabis entrepreneurs. It's one facet of the business world that takes an emotional, exhaustive toll on you and also eats away at your time. Finances can make or break your business as it impacts all the decisions that follow. It's anything but an easy decision. With the stigmas surrounding the cannabis market and the strict regulatory environment, raising capital requires astute attention to the relationships you choose. When embarking on your cannabis business journey, a few financial factors need to be kept in mind, which include:

Your Financial Partner Matters a Lot

Big corporate firms dominating the cannabis industry can be very tempting to partner with. As an entrepreneur, you are eager to partner with investors to be able to scale and pursue high growth opportunities that attract big-name firms. At this point in time, you need to realize that even though the big-name partnerships will help you with your business strategy, your short-term and long-term over-arching vision needs to be synchronized with your partner. Vetting and choosing the right partnership, not just for its name, can have long-lasting risks and a major deal-breaker. Before you sign, DO YOUR HOMEWORK.

Be Prepared with a Precise Pitch to Present to Investors

What that entails is having an oral and visual presentation deck that engages your audience and help you land a lucrative deal with an investor. A great pitch will capture the attention of your audience and a winning first impression. It is imperative that you do your market research and be well-rehearsed about accurate data that will present industry growth opportunities and why your business in the best competitive player in the game. Seasoned investors have an eye for details, and they can discern which companies are worth investing and which ones are a losing bet. Have well-researched knowledge and a revenue-centric business plan to get investors on board. Your pitch and PowerPoint deck represents your business proposal and will be circulated among various investors. Be wise to know that first impressions are lasting impressions – aim to hit the bull's eye.

Know the Worth of Your Business

As a responsible entrepreneur or business owner operating in the dynamic cannabis market, you need to know your business's real value. This is in accordance with the new advancements in the legal cannabis space, as investors have generated an extensive demand. However, as a business owner, you must realize that each round of financing is a stepping stone towards your final goal. The investors only place their bet on your business if they see the value of their investment is proven with time. If investors conduct an evaluation of your business and find hidden risks and inflated costs, they may withdraw at any point in time, or leverage their findings to devalue your company's worth.

Funding and Financing Options for Your Cannabis Business

Bank financing is an almost impossible thing to rely on for a cannabis business as all major banks are under federal government regulations. Since, in the eyes of the federal government, any business venture involved with the dealing of cannabis is viewed as a criminal activity, securing financing from federally chartered banks is out of the question. Even if you want to a loan for business operations, commercial banks can be held accountable under certain federal laws, subject to high penalties. Consider alternative funding resources such as private funding investment, state-chartered and local banks, along with community credit unions. You might get lucky as these alternative financial institutions are far more welcoming to cannabis business owners than big commercial banks. You can take some trust-building measure to help get the support of a bank, as Braden Perry, a specialist in regulatory issues and a regulatory attorney, puts it:

"The key to high-risk areas and banking relationships is to have a strong compliance program and transparency. Independent compliance audits of the company, either by a third party or someone not actively involved in your compliance management system, will add to the trust the bank has with the company."

Having a proper, well-educated, degree-verified HR professional is important at this stage since their prime responsibility is to keep a check on all the laws and Acts regulating the legal and financial environment of the cannabis industry. The Bank Secrecy Act[7] is one of them that directs all federally-controlled banks. These include the smaller ones to deter any transactions that ex-

---

[7] *BANK SECRECY ACT, ANTI-MONEY LAUNDERING, AND OFFICE OF FOREIGN ASSETS CONTROL* https://www.fdic.gov/regulations/safety/manual/section8-1.pdf

ceed the limit of $5000 or more that have any connection with illegal activity. Since marijuana is illegal under federal law, this clause applies to any such transactions carried out through the bank. As a backup plan, here is when you need to have your alternate financing options ready to be able to fund and kick-start your business:

- Equity financing
- Crowdfunding
- Venture Capitalists
- Angel Investors
- Online Lenders
- Debt Funding
- POS System
- Debit System

You can research the requirements outlining these financing options and see what best fits your business models. As profitable as a cannabis business can be, finding the most suitable way to manage your finances comes with its fair shares of struggles, trials, and errors. Due to the wide-scale regulation by the federal government, cannabis business owners and entrepreneurs do not have many options outside of cash. However, some new business startups and local institutions have realized the tough spot that cannabis business owners are in and have stepped in to ease the financial dilemma for them. Just be careful when choosing a financing option for yourself and evaluate all the risks that might be involved before you make a decision.

Know the Industry Holistically

You cannot simply set up a cannabis startup just by growing marijuana. There are several things to determine when considering the prospect of opening up your own cannabis business. Data analytics has progressed by leaps and bounds and can be leveraged to help you create the most impeccable strain to service your customers. Biotechnology and pharma companies have long been in this business and have focused special attention on developing cannabinoid-based drugs.

The cannabis business is full of technology opportunities that can be deployed to help take your business forward. Cannabis market options are not only limited to retail or growing but encompass a lot of other possibilities, such as construction and marketing. The number of various extraction methods and different strains are enough to boggle your mind. With the side effects and legal limitations of cannabis being a constant source of concern, you need to be well aware of all the factors at play. The list is growing every day, and as an entrepreneur, it is your responsibility to stay on top of the trends leading to the cannabis industry. You need to know your cannabis ABCs, CBDs, and THCs. You can elevate your knowledge by joining industry associations, attending conferences, and attending ongoing industry training webinars and seminars.

You may feel that you have gained a command over the basics of Sativa vs. Indica or tested the blend of flavors of every last terp, or learned to appreciate the bliss and the right balance of CBD – but there is a vast amount of knowledge to help you choose which segment is the best fit for you. A desire to establish your credibility should be backed by extensive market research, R&D efforts, classes, and workshops, or any meet up or podcast that can help enrich your knowledge. Connecting with industry thought leaders can also enlighten you on another level.

Here are a few more tips to consider in making a decision about your startup:

Find Your Niche

Like starting any other business, having a business plan and focus requires you to carve out your niche and discover your competitive advantage to distinguish yourself. The cannabis industry will task you to do the same. In fact, the cannabis business is distraught with micro-level regulations that may be deciding factors and may also interfere with your way of doing business and dictating you to follow strict guidelines and policies. Whether you are a part of the plant-touching, growing, manufacturing, selling, or ancillary business – you need to know which one requires certain regulations.

Before you go through any of the financial and legal hassles, know best practices and conduct an audit of what your competitors are doing. Benchmark what they are doing, their strategies, and the industry trends. You can't execute your business plan instantly because opening a cannabis business varies widely for growing cannabis, manufacturing, or opening a dispensary. Choosing your business focus will build momentum and results, which are the rewards of doing your homework.

✓ **Cultivating business:** If you want to venture into cannabis cultivation, you need to have sound knowledge of horticulture and show evidence to get your license. You need to differentiate between different cannabis plant variations based on effect, taste, smell, and many other aspects. Since this part of the industry is directly in contact with growing plants, it is highly regulated and demands a high, upfront investment to purchase the equipment and inventory necessary to set up the facility. The facility where you will cultivate your plant and strain should also meet all compliance and regulatory standards, including state and county bylaws

✓ **Retail sector:** This is one of the most profitable niches in the cannabis industry. Cannabis-based products are sold in facilities called dispensaries of collectives. Retail licensing requires submitting an application, paying a state licensing fee, and patience to wait while your application goes through several regulatory hoops. However, in order to sell to the right consumers, you need to make sure they have a legal marijuana card and not a counterfeit. In compliance with federally and state, and sometimes county control laws, you cannot market your products even on billboards or social media platforms, and verify age limit. Every advertisement has to clearly state age-limits warning and not include language that targets underage youth.

✓ **Manufacturing cannabis-infused products:** This could be a great option to explore as there are many variants rising in this category from marijuana oils, lotions, botanicals, ointments, to cannabis-infused beverages, food, and cosmetics. In 2016, this market grabbed a market share of $180 million in California alone.

✓ **Ancillary business:** if you do not want to undertake the risks that come with the growing, selling, and creating of cannabis products, you can venture into an industry that acts as a support system for the cannabis industry. Options under this category include accounting, human resources, attorney, insurance, payroll, training, real estate, security, tax services, construction, information technology, and transportation.

These are basically the main types of cannabis business licenses that you can acquire. Some states also allow you to register as a cannabis delivery company, laboratory testing, and the like. You need to check that with your state.

Know That You Cannot Write Off All Your Expenses

It should be known to all cannabis entrepreneurs, and business owners that any company dealing in drugs not deemed legal by the federal government cannot deduct anything from "business expense" except for the cost of goods sold. An industry CPA is recommended to complete the business owner's tax return. However, most entrepreneurs are under the impression that to manage their day-to-day expenses and operational costs, they need to be able to write off expenses and boost the bottom-line profits.

However, the legislation ban on cannabis companies was examined when a Minneapolis drug dealer successfully sued the IRS in 1981 to be able to deduct his car, scales, and baggies as "business expenses" on his tax return. Congress then passed new legislation to ban companies dealing in illegal drugs from deducting anything except their costs of goods sold. As a result, this may cost cannabis companies as much as 70% or more in taxes. The IRS Code 280E further complicates things by not allowing businesses who deal in narcotics trafficking and have an income derived from illegal activity to cut ordinary business deductions. As a precautionary measure, if you are a plant-touching business, it is advised that you categorize as many of your expenses under the heading of costs of goods sold (COGS) rather than a general business overhead. Under this law, if you are operating as a storefront and selling recreational or medical cannabis, you may be able to deduct the cost for growing plants but not for the store's rent or the expenses that go in advertising or salaries of the employees. It's worth consulting with legal and tax experts.

Registering and Licensing

State registered businesses dominate the cannabis industry because the federal laws and national prohibitions (no interstate sale of cannabis) discourage a lot of big businesses to venture out into this territory. Operating as a local business on a small scale, you will have to figure out your 'business structure,' which will inevitably determine how you pay taxes and associated risks. You might either want to set up a limited liability company (LLC) or a corporation, coupled with an operating agreement. Both forms safeguard you from owning the entity's responsibility personally, and there are specific tax and organizational features that distinguish the two. This choice will also reflect financing options, such as venture capital, private equity, or to consider a structure for a pre- IPO.

Choosing a name requires you to make sure it is not previously registered and should be state-specific. In most states, you will need to pay a small, up-front fee to reserve the name for your company before you register your business.

The rules for getting registered and obtaining your business license or permit for a cannabis business differs from state to state. There is a range of registrations practices, permits, and business licenses that depend on where you are opening your marijuana business. Joining the NCIA (National Cannabis Industry Association) will help you figure out the rules for your cannabis business.

Taxes and Compliance

Compliance is an arduous and ongoing process that does not really end with you obtaining your state or local level cannabis permits. Certain compliance procedures are essential to maintaining your cannabis licenses. Some basic ideas for why you need compliance include:

- Ensure your location is marked as 'zoned' for the cannabis business that you started
- To maintain your permits and licenses
- Track inventory
- Package and label requirements
- Keep a record and fulfill prerequisites for appropriate documentation
- To maintain HR compliance
- Surveillance and security
- Filing an annual report and paying franchise taxes – for entity-level compliance and LLCs/corporations.

No matter which state you set up your cannabis business, you need to send an application for an Employer Identification Number (EIN), which is also alternatively referred to as a business tax ID number. The application process for the EIN from the IRS is free and can be completed and downloaded immediately online. Legally, an EIN is required and needed to determine your tax structure for your business.

"The most surprising thing about having a cannabis business is the amount of regulation that is involved and how it's constantly changing."

-Dr. Jared Helfant, president of Sparx

The cannabis industry is plagued with a lot of legal and financial loopholes, intricacies, and complications. The best advice would be to have a proper business plan and have all the funding options sorted before jumping into it. Despite the humongous pitfalls, the cannabis industry has innumerable opportunities to cash on for those who have a system to mitigate risk, have an eye for detail, and are ready to embrace the ever-changing legal and regulatory environment with a well-equipped HR function. It can be a highly lucrative endeavor, and you can be one of the cannabis businesses having a slice of the market, which is expected to value in billions in the near future.

CHAPTER 5

HIRING AND ONBOARDING

Looking forward to growing your workforce can be one of the most exciting prospects for a cannabis business, given the plethora of work opportunities abound in the cannabis industry. According to Glassdoor, a job-search website, jobs in the cannabis industry fetch a comparatively higher median salary of $58,511, which is 10% higher than other jobs in various sectors. [8] Given these numbers, more and more people are inclined to apply for jobs in the industry.

The lucrative opportunities make it imperative that the hiring and onboarding process is designed to remove any bottlenecks that might hamper the performance of the business. However, the onboarding process can also prove to be stressful if the right system, modus operandi, and check and balances are not maintained. Whether you intend to take your cannabis business to the next level in terms of opening up a new cultivation plant, setting up a dispensary for vertical integration, or spreading your roots across state lines, fresh talent can always bring a unique perspective to your establishment. This can do wonders for the prosperity,

---

[8] Zhao, D, (2019), *'Demand for Cannabis Talent Heats Up'*

productivity, and, ultimately, the profitability of your organization. As a cannabis business owner, you should realize and acknowledge the fact that employees are your most prized possession. The more your employees feel valued and welcomed, the higher their morale will be.

Building and maintaining a workforce does not end with sourcing, interviewing, and hiring the right person. When the new hire accepts your job offer, the next step is onboarding – which is a comprehensive multi-step process. Your business must take the necessary steps to ensure that compliance requirements are met. Productive and happy employees are the lifeblood of any organization. The onboarding process must be as smooth and hassle-free as possible because that is when the employees get introduced and familiarized with the culture and expectations of the company. An organized procedure is pivotal for both the employee and the company because both have to make an impression on each other to ensure smooth operations. This helps establish a win-win situation as a hiring checklist is made to ensure that all prerequisite checks are in place.

Furthermore, the best practice is for managers to apply the company's onboarding to acclimate, integrate, and transition new employees into the company and their respective new positions. The cannabis industry is fairly new and misunderstood due to the tussle between federal and state law regarding the legalization of marijuana. In such a scenario, maximum efforts must be directed towards team development and training to avoid non-compliance and attract a team of top-notch cannabis professionals that boast professional excellence. Having an HR team that takes care of the hiring and onboarding needs for new employees is essential to build credibility and stay in business in this highly volatile industry.

Many cannabis positions require an insane amount of compliance and relevant knowledge regarding the product, consumer, regulations, system training, and sales procedures. Hiring is just the first step in laying the foundation of a competent and trained workforce. Only when those employees are properly trained, and onboarding programs are implemented do they become an asset to achieve the company's overall vision and goals. Selling cannabis encapsulates many legal complexities and ever-changing regulations that require a well-informed sales team to discharge their duties effectively. Also, the cannabis workforce has to deal with a lot of customer service issues daily and has to be knowledgeable enough to market and sell a diverse range of products without compromising retail or consumer regulations. So, looking at the big picture as a cannabis business owner or entrepreneur, you need to have a strategy to execute your vision while juggling all the industry requirements successfully – it can be done.

Your approach and respect for the industry ultimately get transferred to your employees as they will apply your values and ethics to achieve the company's vision and business objectives. It goes unsaid that for any business idea to reach fruition and bear phenomenal results, you must surround yourself and your business with the right people. You need to understand the challenges and invest the necessary energy and time to get through the legalities and make an offering that is beneficial for both the employee and the organizations.

Make the Onboarding Process Smooth and Hassle-Free

Potential and first-time employees might be intimidated by the onboarding process with the legitimate fear that they might not be able to gel with the company culture. It is natural for some to feel uncertain or unsure if they possess all the required knowledge and skills needed to efficiently and effectively discharge their duties. That is where a robust onboarding process becomes imperative for employees to succeed. Furthermore, the onboarding process should have some salient features that make the employees feel that they are ready to step into a world accepting and conducive to learning. Here are a few recommendations:

- Arrange team-building warm-up sessions with the employees and team to facilitate building rapport.
- Communicate the vision, mission statement, core values, and employee expectations precisely and clearly
- Create a stress-free, relaxing environment
- Give the employees the liberty to choose their path
- Have a mentor to check on their progress constantly

When the onboarding process is smooth, it builds your reputation, and more and more prospective employees will be intrigued and attracted to your business. The manager should make sure that the new employee is introduced to any relevant stakeholders to increase familiarization. There should be no ambiguity regarding the roles and responsibilities of the new position, and the metrics should be properly outlined. When employees join the company, they develop their perceptions, starting on the very first day. An exceptional onboarding experience ensures that your new tribe member feels welcome and valued.

Onboarding is not just an orientation program that is only concerned with the new-hire paperwork but encompasses much more in terms of integrating the new employee in the culture. It involves making sure that the work environment and business processes are well understood, and the new employee has the necessary tools to get on with performing his new responsibilities. Most human resource experts recommend implementing a formal plan that lays down the steps for the onboarding process. The processes involve all the new hires' experiences in the first 90 days in the first year. This prepares them for the profits, losses, and enables them to become a loyal employee by pledging the allegiance and alliance to the company. A lot of recent studies have found a significant positive correlation between a well-thought, holistic onboarding program, and positive results with a 16% improvement in customer retention and a 17% spike in revenue per full-time employee.

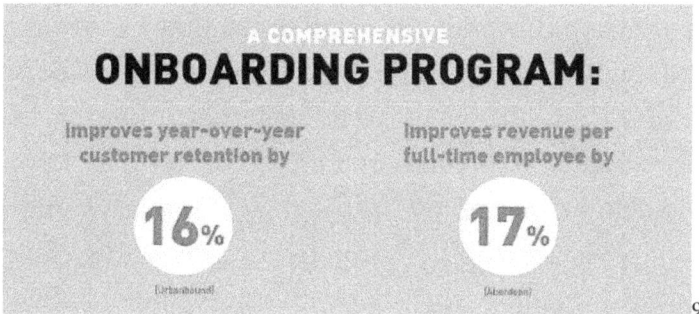

This speaks volumes about how important it is to invest substantial time and energy into onboarding your new hires – it pays higher dividends on the backside. The three primary goals of a well-managed onboarding process are:

Helps them acclimatize

The importance of making the employee feel comfortable cannot be stressed enough. Any employee would take their own time to adjust, but it is up to the employee to set the tone and pace of emersion. To get the employee fully on board and ensure that

---

[9] Deutsch, L (2016), *'Onboarding best practices'*

everyone is on the same page, they must share the vision, are fully aware of what is expected of them, and what role they will play to achieve organizational objectives. Furthermore, new hires also need sufficient supervisory support, coaching, and tools to get things done and regular performance reviews to stay on top of their personal and business goals.

Helps them to engage at a deeper level

Once you've carried out the ice-breaking activities and familiarized the new hires with the existing employees and other stakeholders, it is time to indulge them in more meaningful work. Introduce them to the cannabis industry standards for your specific firm and even establish open door communication between the employee and the upper management. Expectations should be set clearly without any ambiguity, and any expectations that were not met should also be addressed in this stage of creating engagement. When employees are engaged on a deeper level, HR experts have notices that it inevitably translates into customer satisfaction and directly affects bottom-lines.

Retains employees for a longer time

In today's highly competitive economy, it is all the more important to give your employees a chance to align with your company. When the onboarding process is skipped or done haphazardly, it often results in employees leaving the firm because they feel confused and disposable. Your onboarding plan should focus greatly on employee retention. The cost of losing an employee is very expensive; it also involves recruiting, training, and interviewing candidates repeatedly. Some other hidden costs have also been identified, such as reduced morale, lower productivity, and employee disengagement. All of this is lost revenue before you see a net gain and recover your costs and productivity.

The HR function in a cannabis company shoulders a huge responsibility of keeping up with new hire compliance requirements and best practices regarding onboarding when expanding the workforce. That is why it is important for cannabis businesses not to let inexperienced people manage the hiring process, but rather, mobilize this strategy as one of several uniform practices that can be replicated as the business expands its operations. It is essential to ensure continuity across the continuum whether the company is hiring an accountant or a cultivation technician. Complying with the state's employment regulations is an absolute necessity. Further, it is crucial to consider certain employee demographics when hiring individuals from protected classes. For instance, a business with a workforce of more than 50 employees is required to offer FMLA – 'Family and Medical Leave Act' and several other regulations.

Timeliness and Accuracy of the I-9 (New Hire Form)

The I-9 form is one of the most critical steps that need to be taken into consideration for new hires. This form is used to verify the identity of people hired for employment in the US, along with their employment authorization. The form is to be completed within three business days from when a new employee is hired. Employers usually overlook this formality and end up accumulating unnecessary fines. Although not submitting the form on time might seem like a very inconsequential offense, it is nonetheless a breach of the law if it is presented with incomplete details or after the due date. The fields required in this form can be a bit confusing; therefore, hire an expert to do this function. It's always advisable to double-check the details before submitting it.

Developing Functional Job Descriptions

The reason that job descriptions are so important in the cannabis industry is that the jobs in this sector are quite demanding and require a specific skill set to perform duties according to federal, state, and local laws. With so many regulations and policies in place, carelessness mistakes can lead to serious repercussions and hefty fines. Ideally, before you start any new hires, make sure that there is a job description that explains their role and responsibilities, and duties that need to comply with industry standards. They should only be offered the job when they acknowledge that they understand the requirements to the best of their abilities.

Job descriptions are a written outline of the primary functions that a specific job entails and particularly determine whether a particular job role will be successful or not. They set expectations in black and white and help a candidate decide whether they possess the necessary skill set to apply for this job. If any of the candidates do not meet the requirements or prerequisites highlighted in the job description, do not force a fit. The description also includes reasonable clauses such as accommodation for people with disabilities. This is something that is required by some states and federal laws.

Employee Job Classifications and Categories

As a cannabis business owner or entrepreneur, you should be aware of the fact that this industry is not like other industries and requires extra steps to ensure compliance with pay practices and job classifications. The challenges that a cannabis business faces pertaining to governmental laws and legalities are far more complex and novel than those of other industries. When hiring a worker for your company, be clear whether they are classified as an employee or an independent contractor.

Why is this classification necessary and important?

This is primarily because classification determines if you are responsible for:

- Withholding income taxes
- Paying social security
- Paying Medicare taxes
- Or deducting unemployment tax on the wages paid

Under the state and federal wage and hour laws, employees are categorized into two main types:

Exempt employees

Employees who fall into this category are usually the managers, executives, professionals, or outside sales staff along with the administrative staff who are not bound by the overtime provisions of the Fair Labor Standards Act (FLSA). They hold positions that are designed around the criteria and standards of FLSA and the US Department of Labor. Exempt employees are usually salaried professionals.

Non-exempt employees

Employees in this category do work that is also covered under the Fair Labor Standards Act (FLSA). They are entitled to overtime pay for hours worked exceeding 40 hours a week. Non-exempt employees are either paid on an hourly basis or are salaried.

An Employee Handbook Is a Complete MUST

An employee handbook is like a holy hiring guide. Once a business has figured out its formal hiring strategy, documenting it in the form of a comprehensive employee handbook sets the employees' expectations. This handbook includes all the necessary policies, practices, and procedures pertaining to work rules, vacations, and timekeeping, along with any kind of unacceptable performance and behaviors. From employee orientation, review the employee handbook is a good way to establish the company culture and expectations. Your legal counsel should be consulted before rolling out your employee handbook. It is a vital document for every business in the cannabis industry because it also lays down the guidelines and communicates the core values and expectations in clear terms. It can be referred to any time during the onboarding process as well as during the employment tenure. A final piece of advice about the handbook is to ensure all new employees sign this document and make sure that they understand what has been laid down. This is proof that they are taking responsibility for what might happen in the future and can also come in handy when tackling legal lawsuits and disputes, along with any violations of company policies.

Commit to Future of Training and Career Opportunities

As a cannabis company, having differentiators to brand your company as a competitive player in the industry is a way to give your company an edge in a market that has a talent shortage. If your firm has no prior credibility in the cannabis industry, it is highly unlikely you will attract top talent – no one buys an unknown commodity and joins an unknown team.

Today's market is fluid and quickly changing, and people do not want to remain stagnant or stuck in dead-end careers. People are rather looking for job opportunities that encourage competition, growth, and career advancement. With so many cannabis businesses emerging left, right, and center, it is tough to retain great employees and make them feel truly valued. This is why to keep them engaged, and every organization should offer some training opportunities and career advancement to retain talent to compete in the cannabis industry. Some surefire ways to do this are to offer workshops, mentorship, and seminars for your employees to keep them engaged. Most employees prefer professional development over other benefits and would do anything to stay on top of the learning curve.

When you promise your most valuable and hard-working employees the opportunity to grow and advance, your company also advance its competitive edge. A few benefits of business-centric training include:

- In-depth understanding of the job role
- Greater dedication and efficiency on the part of the employees
- Increased loyalty to the company
- Ability to attract consumers and retain them
- An interconnected system of solution-based communications

The onboarding process can make or break your business strategies to build a competitive organization. Likewise, share valuable feedback with your leaders and employees so that they do not feel invested in the business. Remember, the millennial generation operates on inclusion and validation, and there is nothing more gratifying than being valued in an organization.

The hiring process can seem to be daunting on its face, but in reality, it can help you stand out from the crowd. Not every business owner has the sense to ensure that their talent strategy is an investment. Partner with the right recruiting firms, one offers a marketing strategy to attract the best talent. Consider your job descriptions as part of your game plan to master your game to be a competitive player in a highly competitive market. Avoid unnecessary fines and legal lawsuits. If you keep some of these pivotal strategies in mind, you position your company to build a team that will be a billboard for your best practices and leads you towards unprecedented success.

CHAPTER 6

PERFORMANCE MANAGEMENT & TRAINING

"Talent is one of the last frontiers for differentiation. Any company can have a patent or produce a product. The difference is the quality of that product comes with the value of the talent you have."

-Elaine Orler

People in upper management, the board of directors, decision-makers, and influencers now realized how integral performance management is to outperform the competition. Performance management is highly essential to engage employees in a manner that makes them feel valued as part of a larger ecosystem. Regular feedback and performance coaching keep them up-to-date about their valuable contribution and progress in real-time. If any loopholes can be filled to ensure both personal and organizational growth, it is only possible through effective performance management and training.

The performance management system, irrespective of the industry, relies on gathering and monitoring information from reliable sources, tracking key performance indicators (KPIs), with accountability and follow-up. This entire process is done so that the successes and failures are set as a precedent to learn from. This opens up many avenues for learning and growth and helps the business to develop and scale their performance. Talent development follows suit, which helps improve the quality of talent, enhance individual performance, and minimize related problems linked to performance.

With rapid technological advancements and software development, the performance management system (PMS) has become highly automated. This holistic process encapsulated several tools, approaches, and management processes that organizations can take inspiration from. This, in turn, helps you to monitor and manage your employees closely. The human resource department is primarily responsible for ensuring that an effective performance management system is implemented. Just as you set the culture and tone of your workplace, performance management systems are unique to your organization's goals, values, and purpose. Alongside elevating human performance, increasing productivity bottom-lines, and ensuring the well-being of the employees, a well-designed performance management system aims to ensure higher levels of performance, regardless of whether you are an enterprise or a small business. In a way, the business objectives of a firm and performance management are inextricably linked to employee morale, engagement, and wellness.

Performance management is much more than ensuring that your employees are committed and engaged in the workplace using performance appraisals. Poorly performing employees is not only an emotional and physical burden but is also an additional financial cost. It is incumbent upon every employer to make sure that their employees receive the necessary training to develop their skill set to advance their performance for pay and career growth. For training and development objectives to be met, the human resource department monitors the manager's role in evaluating individual and team performance. Here's why performance management systems play an indispensable role in managing and developing employees:

- **It helps predict the future potential of employees** – When you are constantly up-to-date with how your employees are performing and the different ways that you can develop them – it creates a win-win situation for both the employee and the organization. An organization can help mitigate employee risk this way and avoid any future setback by taking control.

- **Identify opportunity for improvement** – performance management gels into development and training strategies and provides clarity in the organization. Employees get to know what is exactly expected of them so that the right people are in the right roles. Often due to lack of communication, expectations are not clearly set, which directly impacts productivity levels.

- **Establishes an open culture that thrives on feedback** – all employee needs constructive feedback and constructive coaching to perform optimally. Complacency and lack of acknowledgment breeds frustration and job dissatisfaction. This inevitably leads to high employee turnover rates. Therefore, effective performance management and training can help retain valuable employees that are considered key talent. Shared communication and feedback also fosters trust and teamwork spirit. Employees feel valued and feel loyal to the company.

- **Increases employee retention and engagement** – performance management becomes part of a culture that recognizes and rewards. Two reasons employees leave and seek other employment is lack of recognition. Employees want to be commended for their hard work but often end up working in a monotonous, robotic routine that does not let them feel a sense of job satisfaction. Engaged employees are more likely to feel loyal to the company. The gap between employees and leaders managed to help employees stay engaged on a much deeper level.

"So, the three qualities of a workplace that would develop people would be information sharing, investing in the training of the workforce, and giving employees the ability to use their training and information to make decisions."

-Jeffrey Pfeffer

The talent management puzzle is a complex one, and performance assessments and appraisals are just one piece of it. In a fast emerging industry like the cannabis market, building an empowered and highly-skilled workforce requires constantly training the talent pool and carrying out necessary employee audits. As the cannabis industry spreads out its roots to encompass local, state, and federal, the landscape is becoming all the more challenging for HR managers to navigate. Retaining employees is a key strategy for the HR function, and finding quality candidates to fill essential roles is a real struggle in this industry. Just 64,000 jobs were added in 2018 in the cannabis industry – another 20,000 jobs were forecasted in the year 2019.

With so many new jobs being created, if employees are not happy regarding their job expectations and satisfaction, shopping for greener pastures is an option for key positions. Job dissatisfaction can also lead to employee burnout when employees feel they are in a dead-end job with the company. Performance management techniques and systems, coupled with learning, take into account performance tracking, offer interactive training courses, provide certifications, and eventually map out success plans that can help employees envision a respectable position in the future.

While training is essential in any organization, it is all the more important in the cannabis industry because of the unique challenges and complex regulations that plague it. If any of the employees are found violating any rules or regulations, your business will bear the brunt. It cannot be emphasized enough that the official onboarding process must be accompanied by a proper, formal set of training that informs the employees on major legal policies and procedures applied to the cannabis market. Your employees must be on the same page regarding the liability that you are shouldering in a highly dynamic and ever-changing industry. The best practice for the cannabis business is to standardize procedures that help mitigate environmental and legal risks. All relevant local and state regulations should be communicated regularly and reinforced through a company's compliance program.

How to Retain Employees in the Cannabis Industry

As your cannabis business grows, managing all aspects of the business becomes all the more challenging, and navigating the legal scenario is almost impossible without a dedicated HR professional to navigate the many industry requirements. Since there are a lot of upfront costs involved in recruiting, onboarding, and training a new hire, retaining high performing employees will help save turnover costs with over a third of the US workers confessing that they want to quit their jobs at some point in time, not only in the cannabis market but many across the spectrum. Employers are plagued with how to keep their workforce engaged and retained over a long span of time.

Unfortunately, recent stats for the turnover rate for retail cannabis employees in Colorado was reported at 62% by a leading cannabis industry platform.[10] The leading reason for the high turnover rate, especially in the cannabis business is primarily due to unrealistic expectations that job seekers hold when it comes to the workplace culture, and career growth in the industry.

Dispensary hopping is a common phenomenon as employees expect advancement in both positions and compensation in an unrealistic time frame. Furthermore, they even expect to be allowed to consume cannabis on-job, which is a violation of one of the basic state laws outlined by most states. Therefore, ongoing training sessions will help employees get to know and understand the industry and company culture more carefully and responsibly. Recruiters are advised to clearly communicate the job expectations and responsibilities in black and white so that there are no unnecessary complications in the future. A realistic preview will help employees evaluate their options before joining any organization. Regular performance reviews can help revisit these expectations and provide updates of any recent laws or regulations that passed in the cannabis market.

Vetting candidates, setting expectations, and arranging an interactive and enlightening onboarding process can make many employees decide to stick with the company past the probationary three-month period.

---

[10] Headset, (2018), *'The Revolving Door Factor: Budtender Turnover in the Cannabis Industry.'*

"For employees to perform at a high level, it only makes sense to include performance management in the onboarding process."

— Sharlyn Lauby

Help them stay on track

Since we have already covered the onboarding process in detail in the previous chapter, I wouldn't go in too much detail. However, I want to reiterate the fact that it is essential to have everyone on the same page. This can be reviewed and revisited regularly and audited for any discrepancies. Evaluate employees' performance and show them how their efforts add value in real-time to achieve company objectives. Make your employees feel appreciated in their role and have them provide diversity and inclusive training to understand differences in communication, leading, and building rapport with diverse people, teams, and, eventually, the entire organization. Do not take your responsibilities or decision making lightly so that your employees feel heard.

Build the Momentum

Employees are on the constant lookout for growth and are not ready to settle for less. If you want to be one of those exemplary employers who offer growth opportunities both inside and outside the company, then you can do so by offering personal development courses and ongoing training. Remember, the millennial generation is yearning for some real growth and efforts made in this regard always bear fruit in curbing high turnover rates. Engaging your workforce is not only a wise move but a necessity to be competitive that requires more than a traditional approach.

Personal development and professional training

Regarding personal development, employees who internalize a heart-felt passion will likely go above and beyond to grow in their skills. A tailored training program helps provide a map for advanced opportunities for career growth and for building company capacity. Having town hall meetings and inviting guest speaker sessions with a cannabis expert can help your employees and leaders stay abreast of the recent developments in the industry. This also helps promote and expand reach to a larger target recruiting audience over a short period. Training courses vary from position to position and are a great way to develop your talent. You can even allocate a budget to your workforce to provide training opportunities because that will only build up your expertise, who is working towards overall organizational development.

PR And Networking

One of the most effective, viable, ongoing retention strategies is providing a platform and opportunity to connect with industry authority leaders. Being connected with the experts help employees stay motivated and build a strong connection that can be leveraged in times of need or to advance career growth. The cannabis industry is a close, well-knit one where major players help others to build a base in a highly volatile environment.

Team Building

Team building and ice-breaking activities help team members to get acquainted with each other. Employee appreciation events and weekend getaways are some examples of informal gatherings that help develop bonding. When you are at ease and comfort with your teammates, you automatically tend to collaborate on a much deeper level – a mega-event every quarter can reinforce the entire culture of inclusivity.

Talent development can also fall under this category as happy employees serve happy customers. In addition to individual skills training, you can also help your employees match the right talent with various vacancies in your organizations. You need to spark that aspiration and inspiration to support employee morale.

Bridge the communication gap

Why are we conducting all those performance assessments and appraisals? For a cannabis company to thrive, it is vital that upper-level management is involved with their teams and are approachable. Besides, employees should always feel connected to an overarching vision and mission. A sense of purpose can be invaluable by inspiring employees to advance their common interests and keep developing new ideas through eLearning solutions. With increased digitalization, getting people connected through an LMS (Learning Management System) is one of the most viable ways to learn and ensure application to improve productivity. Establish the fact that the organization measures are ongoing and monitors at any point in time by conducting surveys and one-on-one sessions. Business owners and CEOs are encouraged to discuss the feedback that you get so that the employees feel heard and know that their opinion is not falling on deaf ears. Loyalty will inevitably follow where there are established, clear lines of communication.

"When feedback is included as part of regular, ongoing performance discussions throughout the year, the employee, the manager, and the organization are all better off."

–Shawna McKnight

Monetary benefits

In the highly competitive cannabis industry, it is all the more important to distinguish your company's competitive pay and benefits. It is known that 22% of employees end up leaving their jobs due to a lack of incentives. This is why a greater number of cannabis companies are elevating their benefits offering in the form of equity, health plans, dental and vision insurance along with paid leaves.

Articulate a sense of ownership

There's nothing quite like the feeling you get when you are in a position where you own your success. Attribute your company's success to that of the employees and share your future aspirations with the workforce. Ask for their opinion on new projects and also keep them up-to-date regarding any milestones achievement. A culture of empowerment helps instill a proactive mindset and supports employees to take the initiative. When you allow employees to associate themselves closely with their work, they are likely to work harder to achieve desired results. They will partake more enthusiastically in training, creating a win-win situation.

Allow Flexibility in Timings and Schedules

Modern problems require modern solutions. With the line between offline and online activities being blurred, employees favor flexible work schedules and environments more than ever. 70% of employees show an inclination towards jobs that offer flexible working schedules, and why wouldn't they? When employees are well-trained and know their worth, they often believe in negotiating their own terms to manage other things simultaneously.

Furthermore, working remotely can drastically lower overhead costs and give people a chance to strike the perfect work-life balance. With greater flexibility from the employer's end, the employee feels a certain level of mutual trust that builds long term relationships. Stress levels are automatically reduced as employees' terms and conditions are being met along with a spike in loyalty and productivity. Could things get any better?

Are you offering your employees the "Cannabis Industry" benefits?

Just when you thought things couldn't get any better, the cannabis landscape provides a unique and exclusive opportunity for businesses of all sizes to set them apart from the rest. With so many big cannabis businesses rising to fame, small cannabis business owners and entrepreneurs need to work smartly to catch up with them. One sure-fire strategy to attract and retain high-quality talent is to tip the scale with extraordinary benefits. These include opportunities to attend cannabis networking events and tradeshow opportunities. Free or discounted products as incentives also receive great traction. Furthermore, you can win over your employees by facilitating them with transportation reimbursement, flexible vacations, day-care services, and a lot more.

"Companies need to shift their approach by creating a culture where regular performance feedback discussions are the norm."
-Melany Gallant

All in all, it would benefit any business owner or CEO to recognize business growth opportunities to invest in human capital and be a part of their journey in an industry that is poised for unprecedented success. Your employees are your most prized assets, and taking out time to develop a strategy to help them will take you and your company to unimaginable heights. It is well worth the investment to go the extra mile to assist your employees comprehensively and holistically. Many of your new hires may be first-time employees and not aware of the details of their first job. To make them feel safe and set them up for success, consider providing an internal mentorship program. Although the cannabis industry continues to face the dilemma of low employee engagement and high turnover rates, programs that promote retention and succession planning can reduce the problem of low engagement and high turnover. Moreover, employees do their research before opting for a career in the cannabis industry or leaving a job for greener pastures.

A multi-pronged approach will curtail the rising level of employee turnover. Although there is no one secret employee retention strategy, effective performance management, compensation, and training can make the employees feel valued. For your effort, identify and attract the right talent, set clear expectations during the hiring process, guarantee the personal and professional success in a dynamic work environment, and retain them through vigorous training programs. Continuous performance management gives managers a valuable view of how well their employees are contributing to organizational goals. It is also a great strategy to identify the high-achievers and boost their morale accordingly. Progress can be tracked against the relevant KPIs, and any shortcomings can be addressed through training and other job enrichment strategies. Important decisions in regards to compensation, bonuses, and appraisals also become more manageable. Not only will this help you build a trusting and reliable workforce but also reduce costs in the long run. Performance management, when done right and well, can maximize ROI and develop an engaged workforce for the long game.

"To be effective and yield results for your business, performance management must be a year-round process with no end."

–Teala Wilson

CHAPTER 7

IS IT TIME TO HIRE AN HR PROFESSIONAL?

Throughout this book, we have analyzed how the cannabis industry has grown exponentially after the legalization of cannabis on a state level. New products and byproducts are emerging in the landscape because of more and more cannabis business owners and entrepreneurs wanting to try their luck to discover other lucrative opportunities. While there is no doubt that the industry has a plethora of opportunities for anyone wanting to scale their business, it comes with its share of challenges that need a dedicated team of HR professionals to keep business owners and CEOs afloat.

The number of employees hasn't grown at the same rate or by the same percentage as the cannabis industry itself. This is because of the strict governmental regulations around employee hiring. With the novel operational challenges and the stigma around the cannabis industry, there's still a long way to go before cannabis business owners can ensure their business's longevity. Cannabis business owners and CEOs are encouraged to take the necessary steps to ensure that their business practices are synchronized with the laws enforced by the state and local government while also meeting national standards. Maintaining compliance is necessary to avoid severe legal actions or fines that may undermine your business name, productivity, and ROI. Adhering to these challenging and highly specific legalities, laws, and regulations require discipline and attention to detail. Someone who has prior knowledge and understanding of the external environment and commands over legal and regulatory matters in the cannabis industry is experienced to handle serious employment concerns that may emerge.

These are in addition to other HR and general business challenges, such as abiding by employment law, staying up-to-date with policies, payroll and employee management, performance management and training, employee retention, and much more. An HR function is specifically set up to tackle everything from attracting the right talent, vetting, hiring, onboarding to employee benefits to making sure your business does not have to pay the price of violating the legalities of the cannabis business.

Outsourcing your HR or hiring an in-house HR team is up to you, but it needs to be in place to help streamline your business across the continuum, resolve interdepartmental conflicts and ensure that business owners and CEOs have the time to concentrate on the core business strategies.

Experience has taught me that the HR administrative burden on emerging businesses can be quite intimidating and put business owners and CEOs in a mentally taxing position. Throughout the book, we have to discuss some fundamental, indispensable, and crucial aspects of HR, without which it is next to impossible for your cannabis business to operate without exposure to risks. Here are some profound signs that will tell you it's time to hire an HR professional.

A non-existent or outdated employee policy manual

It is a misconception in the cannabis industry that only large cannabis companies with several hundred employees need a policy manual. However, any company with more than ten employees becomes liable to have all the proper systems and procedures in place. A few reasons why small cannabis business owners need to be on top of their HR matters and have a well-maintained employee handbook are as follows:

- It is a cornerstone of how compliant and committed your company is to quality standards and practices
- Employees are provided a company document that is intended to help with understanding their job roles, responsibilities, and expectations
- It is a 'go-to" document in times of emergency and helps reduce operational inefficiencies
- It helps prevent the company in defending itself against unfair lawsuits and legal action when the policies are clear.

If you still do not have an employee handbook, it's high time you develop one with the help of an HR professional as it is the best protection against breach of policies and procedures. It also helps develop a productive workforce and is a source of guidance for new hires.

Not up-to-date with the recent laws and regulations

A lack of a proper and well-established HR function can drain valuable time and momentum, where having an HR professional can manage all aspects of this function to support the business strategies. Not only do laws undergo constant amendments and updates, but they also differ widely from state to state. Some of the important employment laws include the Fair Labor Standards Act (FLSA), the Health Insurance Portability and Accountability Act (HIPAA), and the Family and Medical Leave Act (FMLA). It is not humanly possible to stay on top of all these laws while managing the company's growth.

Owning a cannabis business is no small feat. You have to keep yourself legally insured and licensed so that you can furnish proof of your credibility if you ever involved in a legal lawsuit. Several other eligibility prerequisites and criteria also exist. One such example is the necessary condition for all Californian dispensaries to have an ID badge to locate their employees, have alarm systems in place, constant security personnel, 24-hour video surveillance, and commercial grade locks.

Laws in the cannabis industry are also big on health and safety standards. Having a safety plan for occupational hazards and ongoing training is required for plant-touching, processing, security, and transportation providers. If your company doesn't provide adequate training to employees regarding safety protocols, it is highly likely that you, as a business, are violating OSHA Job Safety and Health laws. If you are found breaching any of these laws, and an employee gets hurt at your workplace, your company will be held liable, and you will have to undergo certain legal mitigations that can undermine your business.

These are some glaring signs that it is time to hire an HR so that they can navigate the legal landscape with ease and keep themselves updates regarding the state, federal and local laws and know what steps to take to ensure compliance. Without a dedicated team to handle these legalities, you increase your litigation risk profile and are unable to implement any cost-saving compliance strategies.

Offering Employee Benefits Is Out of The Question Due to Rising Costs

Although setting up and maintaining an HR function might seem like a lot of work and a major expense, cannabis business owners and CEOs should really evaluate the benefits that it offers your company. An HR team keeps a check on unnecessary administrative costs that drain the company of its valuable resources. When HR is there to take care of general administrative and HR-related tasks, the other departments can concentrate on their core competencies, thus removing this burden. These savings allow companies to invest in employee benefits – which is one of the most sought-after incentives by cannabis employees. These include health savings plans, medical insurance, paid leave, flexible work schedules, and retirement plans.

Four out of five employees would rather opt for perks and benefits than a pay raise to feel valued. A 401(k) plan is the equivalent of one in the top five most preferred employee benefits. However, most plan providers also conduct background checks when getting involved with a cannabis company. If the cannabis business does not have a proper HR system in place, they consider the risks and potential legal exposure that may tarnish their brand.

Furthermore, cannabis startups that are comprised of less than ten employees are not targeted by plan providers because they do not seem to be many small companies that are not considered lucrative enough to make profits. An HR expert can provide other strategies to attract the right talent for the right job. Whether you have a small and mighty team or a tribe, great talent is a commodity that represents your company's brand. To manage operating

RENZIE L. RICHARDSON

costs, more employers are getting creative with benefit plans and still attract top talent.

Employee Training Is Neglected

We have talked at length regarding the importance of training for development and compliance. In the absence of an HR expert, the company is shortfalls that are linked to skills, competencies, and development. With imposed excuses that there is no time to train, the results are talent erosion, turnover, and disengagement.

Furthermore, although training standards are inconsistent across the spectrum, this does not exempt employers from implementing required training and annual training requirements to minimize conduct that is considered harassment or discrimination. When an employee receives ongoing education and training, productivity, and revenue targets increases. The need for an HR professional becomes all the more important here so that employees can be trained as per their current status. Training can be broadly categorized into three types:

Basic training – deals with anti-discriminatory and anti-harassment laws and other over-arching company policies.

Continuing education – entails equipping the employees with the necessary knowledge updates, skills, and tools to better job performance.

Corporate training-introduction on new or improved laws abound the cannabis industry, new company procedures, and processes.

Considering a dispensary business in the cannabis industry, your employees serve at the front end of your business. This requires dispensary employees not only to be well-versed about cannabis products but also to have constant updates on state regulations that are often updated and understanding the dispensary operations. Your employees are the face and part of the company's brand, and one of the most important responsibilities is to present your business in the best possible light. Having relevant knowledge will make it easier for them to serve and educate your customers on your line of products and services. Knowledge such as understanding potency, application, and doses is pivotal to offering customers with the right information, and only training can help your staff holistically serve the customers and understand what they can advise and is considered medical advice. This greatly reduces liability and keeps your staff safe from illegible transactions. An HR expert knows the importance of developing employee training programs that cover required and development training. The investment in training will provide tangible results that impact positive revenue growth. HR ensures that all employees have access to continuing education programs, skills development, and leadership development, starting with sourcing, recruiting, and onboarding the right talent. Closing this gap in the organization is key to elevating the company for accelerated growth.

Is Your Employee Turnover High And Costing You Profits?

Do employees find it hard to have an alliance and allegiance with your organization? Do employees end up leaving before the 90 days? Or is it generally hard to find and hire great talent in the cannabis industry? It might not occur to you right away, but hiring the right person for the right job can prove to be the wisest investment in your business's success. Not everyone has the skill sets to work in a grow room and directly handle cannabis plants. Sound, technical knowledge is of utmost importance. If you do not have a proper HR system to deal with the hiring and screening protocols, employees come and go through a revolving door. Besides, leaving current employees overburdened due to new employees entering and exiting the organization in a matter of weeks or months leaves them constantly juggling their job responsibilities and added responsibilities due to job vacancies.

The result is burnout, stress, and feeling negatively about the company. A vigorous screening and interviewing procedure ensure that the best hiring decisions are made, and sub-par candidates do not enter the system. As a cannabis business owner, when you are the one making all the decisions, it is but natural to experience time delays in production, operational inefficiencies, and a compliance lag. All this portrays your organization in a negative light, and lack of a formal system deters your momentum and progress. With HR as a business partner, they manage the training and talent management strategies to be implemented right from the employee's induction to the exit interview. The HR professional takes away the hassle of training and talent management by recruiting top-notch quality talent through comprehensive job descriptions, screenings employees, performing all the necessary background checks, selecting and compensating them accordingly.

Disorganized and Inaccessible Employee Records

Nothing could be more indicative of a lack of an HR function than the inability to maintain employee records and locate important information when needed properly. It is industry best practice to have a personnel file for each employee of the organization, with a HIPPA-protected folder containing sensitive information such as worker's compensation, medical-leave information, and other benefits. A valid I-9 form completes the file and should always be accessible to the ICE (Immigration and Customs Enforcement) and furnished in accordance with employer requirements. Incomplete or missing I-9 forms can cost your business thousands of dollars in fines and legal litigation procedures. The HR function responsibly takes care of all the documentation and ensures that any missing documents be provided so that there are no gaps in the systems. Specific policies and required training need the employees' signature, which is a standard to avoid unnecessary fines and lawsuits.

How Hiring an HR Professional Will Give Your Company the Competitive Edge Over Others?

With cut-throat competition and a constantly evolving legal environment, having a competitive advantage means equipping your leaders and employees to differentiate themselves from other market players. This helps set the bar high for quality expectations, reduced costs, and higher innovation. Sometimes, this competitive edge drives sales and helps the company to scale, achieve sustainability, and success. Several strategies can be leveraged to set yourself apart, but the one in which your human capital is developed has no comparison. After all, employees are the lifeblood of your organization, and you wouldn't ever be able to elevate your performance with great leaders and employees. The business objectives determine where you need to develop a competitive advantage so that it is leveraged as superiority and dominance over others.

Optimizing and Maximizing Operations

Any business aiming either to achieve quantity, quality, or efficiency needs to make sure that the right talent is hired for the right position. If people are in the right position with sound knowledge regarding job duties, the chances of achieving those business goals increases. As an advantage, these critical players should be mobilized using a workforce plan that will guide them towards achieving the target objectives. This is solely what an HR professional does. This role identifies the gaps in the talent pool and addresses them before they become gaping holes in the organization. It is the responsibility of every HR expert to liaise with the company leaders and work in close tandem with company employees to create a win-win goal. These employees can be either developed internally, exposed to international training, or advanced to become an intrapreneurial source to grow and duplicate the brand in new locations or regions.

While technical skills hold their own importance, human resources are all about selecting, developing, and training talent with a unique skill set. Their strengths and traits help them take the lead in bringing about positive change. A few indispensable traits to create a productive workforce are a blend of traits that include creativity and innovation, self-direction, agility, flexibility, controlled risk-taking, adaptability, result-oriented, high level of engagement, responsibility, and accountability. The selection process should start with the company's talent profile and a set of parameters so that applicants are screened and selected against the company talent profile. Existing employees can also be evaluated against the company talent profile as employees develop and evolve their skills in part for succession planning and intrapreneurship.

In the end, no matter how much capital you invest in your company or how many years you take to be a major player in your market, if you do not take your human resource needs seriously, you are setting your company for marginal growth. As a cannabis business owner, CEO, or entrepreneur, understanding your human capital's value will take you to greater heights when you invest in them with genuine intentions. If you support their own personal development, they will invest their performance towards organizational goals. Your employees are your competitive edge. There is nothing more viable partnering with a human resources professional to support the front line staff, back-end staff, executive-level leaders, mid to senior-level directors, and the management C-suite. HR initiates and facilitates new ideas, problem-solving, and encouraging innovation and collaboration. A sound HR professional understands and acknowledges all the challenges that a cannabis business faces on various fronts. Your HR strategies are a reflection of your core values and beliefs, and there should be no compromise regarding it.

Develop the right HR strategies to appeal to the right talent and train them to be a competitive advantage for your business. Not only do the ever-changing laws and industry standards directly influence operational success, but they also help dissolve the stigma around the cannabis industry. It is best to have an in-house HR resource or partner with an outsource firm, HR complexities are best managed by an expert who knows their industry and the job.

My advice to all business owners, CEOs, and entrepreneurs is to avoid HR malpractices and taking short cuts that will backfire and may cost you your entire business or hefty fines. The HR landscape is filled with various challenges, but if you are determined in your approach, one effective way to mitigate your risk is with a highly trained and talented leadership team and workforce.

Hiring an HR professional is an asset – not a liability.

www.ingramcontent.com/pod-product-compliance
Lightning Source LLC
Chambersburg PA
CBHW030532210326
41597CB00014B/1117